Old SELKIRK

by
Alex F. Young

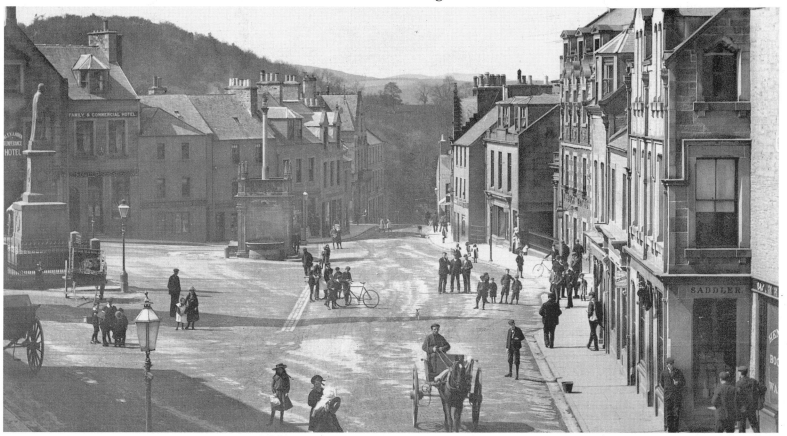

Market Place, viewed from High Street around 1903. On the left, beyond the Sir Walter Scott statue, is the Alexandra Temperance Hotel (manager – Charles Reekie), with a medley of buildings running down to the West Port. On the right is Henderson's boot warehouse, George Stewart the saddler's and the Fleece Hotel (manager – William Gilbert).

Text © Alex F. Young, 2005
First published in the United Kingdom, 2005,
by Stenlake Publishing Ltd.
Telephone: 01290 551122
www.stenlake.co.uk
Printed by Cordfall Ltd., Glasgow, G21 2QA

ISBN 1 84033 357 X

ACKNOWLEDGEMENTS

The author wishes to thank Walter Bryson, Cathy Chick, Michael J. Christie, Robert Croall, Wat Currie, Catherine Dickie, Sam Laurie, Jack Low, Eric Middleton, Ian Mitchell, Ann Plowman, Harry and Sheila Turnbull, Edith Scott and Susan Windram of the *Southern Reporter*, and the Scottish Borders Archive and Local History Centre, Selkirk. The publishers wish to thank Mrs Caroline Cruikshank for permission to reproduce the photographs on pages 6, 23, 28 and 29; and Mr Eric Paterson for permission to use the advert on page 28.

FURTHER READING

The books listed below were used by the author during his research. Only one of them is available from Stenlake Publishing. Those interested in finding out more are advised to contact their local bookshop or reference library.

William Angus, *Ettrick & Yarrow; A Guide*, pub. James Lewis, Selkirk, 1894.
George Chalmers, *Caledonia, A History of Caledonia*, pub. Alexander Gardner, Paisley, 1887.
Alasdair Wham, *Borders Railway Rambles*, Stenlake Publishing Ltd, Catrine, 2004.
The Topographical, Statistical and Historical Gazetteer of Scotland, pub. A Fullarton & Co., London & Dublin, 1847.
The Statistical Account of Scotland, Vol. 2, pub. William Creech, Edinburgh, 1792
The New Statistical Account of Scotland, Vol. 3, pub. Wm. Blackwood & Sons, Edinburgh & London, 1845.
The Third Statistical Account of Scotland; The Counties of Peebles & Selkirk, Bulloch & Urquhart eds., pub. Collins, Glasgow, 1964.

INTRODUCTION

In her book, *A Companion and Useful Guide to the Beauties of Scotland* (published in London in 1803 under the pseudonym of Mrs Murray), the Hon. Sarah Aust (1744–1811) writes of finding Selkirk, '. . . truly deplorable. The houses are mostly old, falling to pieces and deserted: nothing but dirt and misery to be seen.' Up to this point, perhaps Mrs Murray had been paying too much attention to the 'Beauties' to have noticed the towns – Selkirk was far from unique.

Almost contemporary with this account is the Rev. Thomas Robertson's submission to the *Statistical Account of Scotland* – 'The town of Selkirk is pleasantly situated on a rising ground, and enjoys an extensive prospect, especially up and down the River Ettrick . . .' – and, almost in answer to Aust, he also noted that there '. . . is no place in the country so free from epidemical diseases . . . . There are a good many from 70 to 80, three at and above 90, and one died lately at 106.'

By then the town had formed around its 'triangle' – still found at its heart today – running from the West Gate, through the Square with its tolbooth, along High Street where it turned sharply into Well Wynd and Back Raw, returning to the Square along Knowe Heid and Kirk Wynd. The sprawling town developed during the Industrial Revolution and would have been hard to defend in earlier times.

By the time of the Rev. Robertson's account, Selkirk's traditional cottage-based industries of spinning and weaving – with the work distributed by agents from elsewhere – would soon be over with the building of new water-powered mills for both spinning and weaving. Earlier industries had included an inkle-factory, producing the broad linen tape used to trim clothing, a tan work, a small fulling mill, for the scouring and beating and hence cleaning of woollens, and some stocking looms. Nature had provided the elements for Selkirk's future as a manufacturing centre – miles of moorland to support sheep and the Ettrick Water to power the mills to card, spin and weave. Finally, in the 1830s, came man's contribution – a road to Edinburgh and a marketplace. The town council also played their part, building the cauld and the lade that would power the mills. When, in 1838, they decided to dispose of the system at auction, hoping to realise £40, it was knocked down at £210. By the end of 1836 the Ettrick Mills and the Dunsdale Mills were in operation and the following year, Forest Mill.

Each successive decade brought another mill and, with the coming of the railway in 1856, Selkirk goods were reaching an unlimited marketplace. But the mills needed labour and between 1841 and 1851 Selkirk's population almost doubled, rising from 1,675 to 3,314. This increased population required housing. Initially new house building (mainly for rental) was confined to vacant ground in the 'old town', but later came new developments around Knowepark to the north and Heatherlie to the south. The problem would be ongoing and the largest single area of housing was developed at Bannerfield, where 266 houses were built between 1949 and 1963.

With their hours in the mills long and laborious, and at times dangerous, it is little wonder workers took to sport in their leisure time – rugby, soccer and curling in winter, or cricket, bowls and golf in summer – each sport having its own league or cup, with teams from each mill or made up from other workers, including the shopkeepers.

A lot has happened to Selkirk in the two centuries since Ms Aust wrote her caustic comments. What would she think coming into Market Place today? Indeed, what does the stranger arriving today think? Well, that depends on their experience, and where they live. Many from the old Scottish coalfield area – from Ayrshire to Fife – will not believe the loss Selkirk suffered with the closure of the mills until they see the derelict hulks lining Dunsdale Road, so prosperous does Market Place and the streets around appear.

Opposite: A view of High Street running from Market Place, again from the early years of the twentieth century. Of the business names that can be picked out are James Elliott & Son (agents for Melrose's Celebrated Teas), founded in 1846 when James came to Selkirk from Traquair as a 27-year-old (he was succeeded by his son Alexander), George Stewart's saddler's, the drapery premises of Kirkcudbrightshire-born Peter H. Lidderdale, and the County Hotel (manager – William Johnstone).

An 1894 advertisement for coach tours from the County
Hotel to St Mary's Loch and Moffat, with the option of
returning to Selkirk by rail from Innerleithen.

The County Hotel on High Street in the early 1930s. Dating
from the early nineteenth century, when it traded as The
Grapes, it was later remodelled with a Victorian frontage
and given the new name. Horse-drawn carriage tours,
especially down the Ettrick and Yarrow valleys, would run
for many more years, but by 1906 the hotel was a member
of the (Royal) Scottish Automobile Club and the
Automobile Association and listed in the Michelin Guide,
in which the following tariffs were given: Room: 5/-;
breakfast in Coffee Room: 3/6; Lunch: 3/6; and Dinner:
5/-. It had adjacent garaging at 2/- per night and the
services of a chauffeur were available at 12/- per day.

Market Place in 1921 with the 110-feet spire of the Courthouse-cum-Town Hall – built in 1803 to replace the Tolbooth in the Square – towering over Sir Walter Scott's statue. Part of the town hall building was the premises of the flesher, Robert Turnbull, who specialised in salt beef and pickled tongues. The town clock was installed in 1870 and illuminated for the first time on the evening of Saturday, 3 September, that year. In the right foreground is the Pant Well – 'pant' being derived from the eighteenth-century southern Scots word for a public well, fountain, or 'puddle by a midden'. Its history is poorly recorded but apparently in 1715 Sir William Scott of Thirlestane gifted a water trough for the natural spring, and in 1765 this was enlarged and repaired with stone from the demolitions then going on around Market Place. The town's arms and the column from the old mercat cross were added later. The present edifice was built in 1898 to mark Queen Victoria's Jubilee, using a design by the Edinburgh architects John More Dick Peddie (1853–1921) and George Washington Browne (1853–1939), who also designed Edinburgh's Caledonian Hotel. The Pant no longer serves as a checkpoint for the water supply to the lower part of the town.

On a pedestal carrying the arms of the Scott family, the arms of Selkirk, a winged harp and a Scots thistle, the 1839 statue of Sir Walter Scott (1771–1832) was executed by the Mussel-burgh-born sculptor, Alexander Handyside Ritchie (1804–1870). So much has been written of Scott's public persona and his legacy to the Borders area, there may be little left to say that is fresh. But was there another side to the man? To the young Queen Victoria's query regarding extend-ing education to the poor, her prime minister, Lord Melbourne (1779–1848), responded by quoting Scott – 'Why bother the poor? Leave them alone!'. Behind the monument, extending right from Flesh Market Street (previously Fleshmarket Close), with its signpost for the Waverley Stables, were the premises of Thomas Turnbull (b. 1853), the wine and spirit merchant; the poulterer, game dealer and fish merchant, George Hall (who had succeeded Robert Simpson); and the Merton-born baker, Robert Douglas.

Residents old and young pose for the photographer in Tower Street as it rises from High Street to Back Row and beyond on its way to Hawick. In 1714 it was Wintrop's Close and on Wood's map of 1823, New Road. Its appearance here as a residential street with a few shops – Robert Hardie the tailor and clothier and Galashiels-born Mary Oliver's china and fancy goods shop on the left – is deceiving. In 1910 it held at least seventeen other businesses, including Robert Laidlaw the blacksmith, John Blair the butcher, the engineers and cycle agents Stark and Murray, and Symington's wash house and laundry. The buildings on the right were replaced by flatted housing in the 1960s.

In the early 1850s the enterprising, West Linton-born, provisions
merchant, George Lewis (1825–1907) bought the printing firm of
Australian gold rush-bound Thomas Brown for £40, and within
months was publishing a free advertising sheet – the *Selkirk Advertiser*
– with snippets of news in the column space not sold to advertisers.
The step to a true newspaper came on 6 October 1855 with the first
edition of the monthly *Southern Reporter*. In the 1870s, by which time
he was living at Vicarsknowe on the Glebe, his sons James and John
joined the business as, respectively, a bookseller and a compositor.
The newspaper, today part of the Tweeddale Press Group, moved to
the Hermitage in 1990 and from hot metal to full computer technology
in 1995.

Despite much apathy and opposition, the £800, three-storey, 'working men's club', the Selkirk Institute on High Street, was finally opened in January 1911 by Sheriff Patrick Smith. With a reading room, games room (draughts, chess, dominoes and cards – but no gambling), baths, committee rooms, and – to the rear – a 65 feet by 24 feet, four-table, billiard hall, ringed with raised seating, membership was 3/- per annum and its popularity immediate. At the first annual meeting, held eight months later, the accounts showed a credit balance of £12. Membership fees had brought in £49 and the billiard tables £123 15s. 4d. The bronze plaque between the ground floor windows, to the memory of Tom Scott R.S.A. (1854–1927), who was born in the house, was superseded by a first-floor level bust and granite memorial which was funded by public subscription.

The end of High Street, from Agnes Haldane's confectionery shop, the Selkirk Picture House Company's cinema (later bought by Alnwick Playhouse Ltd, The Hippodrome, Workington) down to the Co-op on the Chapel Street corner, and on the right Mungo Park's (chestnut) Tree, planted when the ground was Dr Alexander's garden. The 800-seat Picture House opened on Friday, 1 January 1915, with a continuous programme – from 3.00 p.m. until 10.30 p.m. – featuring the 'sensational war drama', *A Daughter of Belgium*, a Keystone comedy, *The Fatal Mallet*, and a 'fine patriotic film', *England's Call*, which was dedicated to Lord Kitchener (1850–1916). These were all interspersed with 'The Latest War News In Pictures, And Other Good Subjects'. As elsewhere at this time, visits to the Picture House became part of life in the town. The admission prices were: Pit, 3*d*. (children, 2*d*.); Stalls, 4*d*. (2*d*.); Balcony, 6*d*. (3*d*.) and 9*d*. (4*d*.). The cinema closed on Saturday, 6 February 1971, its final show a screening of *Born Free*. Almost within days it was demolished and the site was taken by a Templeton's supermarket.

The High Street/Back Row junction, with the Mungo Park monument, the Municipal Buildings, and Walter Bryson's garage under the shadow of the United Presbyterian Church's 130-feet spire (now the Lawson Memorial Church). The Park monument was designed and carved by the Ettrick Bridge (Howford)-born sculptor Andrew Currie (1813–1891), probably at his studio at Darnick, Melrose, in 1859. The Ettrick monument at St Mary's Loch and the Bruce statue at Stirling Castle are also by his hand. The bronze panels of Park's travels in the Niger area of west Africa, by Thomas Clapperton, were added in 1905, and the life-size figures, representing Peace, War, Slavery and Home Life in the Niger, again by Clapperton, in 1913. Left of the Municipal Buildings, behind the statue, is Walter Bryson's Municipal Garage. Established around 1905, he was the local agent for Argyll and Ruston–Hornby cars, and his premises had indoor parking for 20 cars, including six for hire, offered 24-hour service seven days a week, and boasted the modern facilities of an inspection pit and the ability to recharge accumulators (batteries). In 1923 both he and the Selkirk Motor Co. on Ettrick Terrace had a petrol pump installed. There was also, at this time, Paterson Bros.' Victoria Garage on Buccleuch Road. Bryson amalgamated with Croall & Croall of Kelso in 1928 to become Croall Bryson Ltd.

Selkirk Co-operative Society's buildings at 74 High Street, rounding into Chapel Street, opposite the Victoria Hall, around 1908. Its registered office was at 7 West Gate. Founded in 1846, by the time of this photograph Selkirk had share capital of £23,319 and 48 employees, generating sales of £43,416 to its 1,087 members, who each received a dividend of 3/4d. in the pound on an annual profit of £8,069.

A horse and cart of William Scott the baker of High Street – the driver with his whistle and money bag – out on its daily rounds. Selkirk at this time, around 1906, had four other bakers – Robert Hope, also in High Street; Robert Douglas and Sinclair & Christie in Market Place; and the Co-op.

Here still under construction, Selkirk's public hall was later named Victoria Hall to commemorate the Queen's 1897 Jubilee. Building began with the laying of the foundation stone in October 1895 by Mrs A.F. Roberts, wife of woollen manufacturer Alexander F. Roberts. Erected at a cost of £6,150, in a 'blousy renaissance style' by the Edinburgh architect Hippolyte J. Blanc (1844–1917), it was built of red sandstone from Cumberland's Moat Quarry and faced with red stone from Edinburgh's Hailes Quarry. On 6 May 1899 the Duke of Buccleugh handed the hall over to the town. Blanc also designed the Masonic Hall (1897) in Back Row. Later came the Fletcher Memorial, by Thomas Clapperton, to celebrate the quatercentenary of the Battle of Flodden, and the memorial, on the corner of Chapel Street, to the life of J.B. Selkirk (1832–1904). Born at Galashiels in 1879, Clapperton trained at art colleges in Glasgow and London and though known for his war memorials, he also sculpted the 1929 statue of Robert the Bruce on the Esplanade at Edinburgh Castle.

Ettrick Forest Bowling Club green and clubhouse in the early twentieth century. There are two accounts as to the club's foundation and opening in 1876. The first relates that when the bowling green at Philiphaugh, to which estate employees had access one evening per week, was converted to a tennis court in 1874, Sir William Strang Steel purchased this land at Thorniehall Nursery on Scott's Place and gifted it to the foundling Ettrick Forest Bowling Club. He also gifted four sets of bowls. However, according to a contemporary *Southern Reporter* article on its opening, '. . . about the end of 1874, a few of the working men in the town thought they might endeavour to form a bowling green . . . and the land was feued from Mr Anderson of Broomhill, who gifted the first year's feu rent.' The clubhouse and pavilion shown here was superseded by the one ravaged in a fire of April 2002. The roller was given to the cricket club.

Sheriff Patrick Smith (1858–1930) of The Firs, David C. Alexander of Thirladean (skip), Adam Grieve of The Glebe, and Alexander F. Roberts of Fairnalee on the ice at Selkirk Curling Club's rink at Thorniehall on Scott's Place (previously Thornyhall Nursery and now the car park adjacent to the police station). The photograph was taken on their return from Kanderstag, Switzerland, where they won the World Curling Championship in February 1906. Officially founded in November 1850, with the Duke of Buccleuch as patron, the club had used Headshaw and Haining Loch before coming to Scott's Place. Their other successes included winning the Border Tournament Trophy outright in 1885 and taking gold at the first England v Scotland curling match, at Carlisle in 1895, with the team comprising William Grieve (replaced by Patrick Smith for the team to Switzerland), Alexander F. Roberts, Adam Grieve and David C. Alexander. Climate change forced the game indoors, firstly to Haymarket Ice Rink, Edinburgh, from 1913, and then, from 1964, Kelso's Border Ice Rink.

Dovecot Park, viewed from Scott's Place end, with the trees of Thornyhall Nursery on the left, and the four semi-detached Dovecot Cottages on the right. The houses beyond were built between 1856 and 1880. On the right of the picture, standing in the cottage doorway in her white apron, is Mrs Elizabeth Henderson, then well into her sixties. She traded as a confectioner and fruiterer from a room in the cottage. She and her late husband Robert, a mill watchman, had raised two sons, Robert and Alexander, and two daughters, Elizabeth and Jane, in this house. The street was named after Dovecot House, the one time home of Dr Henry Scott Anderson, who was provost in the 1870s.

A view of Curror Street taken in the summer of 1912, with Knowepark School – built at a cost £3,763 and opened on 4 January 1882 – just visible on the left, sweeping down from Bleachfield Road towards Charley's Brae (possibly named for Charles Brodie, the 1818-born woollen dyer and councillor, who lived at number one). The street and school were part of the town's 1870s expansion to accommodate the influx of mill workers. The coalman is not known, but at that time there were seven in the town. Up to the 1860s they were based around the railway station – the coal arriving by train – but later spread their business premises throughout the town.

The West United Free Church on Ettrick Terrace, photographed shortly after the appointment of James A. Somerville as minister (he served between 1904 and 1925). At the Disruption within the Church of Scotland in 1843 some 200 ministers and their congregations left the established Church, and in Selkirk those who left the Lawson Memorial Church had built this church, seating 490, by 1850. In 1963 the West Church congregation joined St Mary's and the county council used the building shown here until regionalisation in 1975. Having fallen into disuse it was demolished in 1983, although the gateposts remain.

Raeburn Road – Raeburn Place from 1932 – as it climbs towards the Infectious Diseases Hospital, photographed from Shawburn Toll in 1913. The centre of the road marked the new north boundary of the Burgh of Selkirk when it was extended under the provisions of the General Police and Improvement (Scotland) Act of 1862. In the 1880s it had only three houses, but development was soon underway.

The view down Raeburn Road to Dunsdale Woollen Mill on Dunsdale Road, before the widening of the main road swept away Shawburn Toll House, the small cottage in the centre of the picture.

Buccleuch Road looking to Station Road and Forest Mill, with Victoria Park on the left, in the summer of 1914. 'Forrest' Mill, as it appears on Mitchell's map of 1851, was built after October 1838 by George Roberts and Andrew Dickson on land bought from the burgh council which was once the site of Walter Hog's small hosiery business. On the right are the premises of licensed grocer William Park, who came to Selkirk from Dalkeith in the early 1880s. Initially, he would have lived above the shop, but by the 1890s had moved to the house Glenesk in The Glebe.

An 1894 advertisement for William Park's shop.

A brougham hire cab outside McLean's shop in the Buccleuch Building on the corner of Station Road and Buccleuch Road. The railway station entrance was opposite and the house on the right was part of Bridgehaugh (yarn) Mill. The Buccleuch Building was erected in 1875 and for a time was occupied by the printer and bookseller, William Crichton, before being taken by James Colin McLean who ran it as a newsagent, sub post office, telegraph office, bookseller (with lending library), music seller, stationer and tobacconist until his death in 1923. He had the town's first telephone installed (Selkirk 1). In early days the corner was a meeting place, becoming crowded after 6.00 p.m. by those awaiting arrival of the Edinburgh train carrying the *Evening News* and *Evening Despatch* newspapers. The business was run by McLean's son, John, until the early 1960s, when he was succeeded by his son-in-law, Robert Dickie. Only in 1993 did the business pass out of the family's hands. The fly sheet on the wall reads 'North Cumberland; Who Is Mr Claud Lowther's Successor?'. This dates the photograph to the autumn of 1922, when, in the run up to the November general election, Claud W.H. Lowther (who had been elected in 1918 as a Coalition Conservative (Independent) MP) announced that he would not be standing for re-election.

An advertisement for Dorn's Station Hotel on Station Road, following its refurbishment in the early 1890s. The 1901 census shows the proprietor as 39-year-old, Bavarian-born (naturalised British) John C. Dorn, who lived in the hotel with his 31-year-old, Leith-born wife, Mary and their six-year-old daughter, Leonore. By 1910 the Dorn family were gone and William Wilson had taken over.

Selkirk Railway Station on a quiet day. Opened on 5 April 1856 – the first train having completed the journey on 25 March – by the Selkirk & Galashiels Railway (absorbed by the North British Railway in 1859), the six-and-a-half-mile line to Selkirk branched off the Edinburgh to Carlisle line (the 'Waverley Route') one mile east of Galashiels, calling at Abbotsford Ferry (for visitors to Scott's house at Abbotsford) and Lindean on the way. The first turf of the station building was cut by Provost George Roberts and Sir John Murray of Philiphaugh. The railway transformed Selkirk, being not only a conduit for the town's industry – bringing in raw materials and cheap coal for the mills, and taking out its manufactured goods – but also enabling the townspeople to travel more extensively and allowing travellers to visit more easily.

The end of the line, with the engine sheds to the right and the platform on the left. By the late 1940s increased road traffic had reduced train services from ten to two per day and the service was axed in September 1951. Goods traffic continued until 1964.

The Corn Mill on Station Road, with the bridge over the mill lade on the right, shortly before its demolition in 1901, when it was replaced by the water pumping station. The last miller is thought to have been William Ewing, who is listed in an 1897 directory. Amongst the posters on its gable is one for the forthcoming attraction, *Sherlock Holmes*, a world-renowned play produced by the Ben Greet Company (founded by the actor-manager Sir Phillip Barling Ben Greet, 1857–1936). Fresh from London's Lyceum Theatre, its next performance would be in the Victoria Hall.

Opposite: The West Port, looking towards Market Place, in 1909. On the right is the local branch of the National Bank of Scotland (founded in Edinburgh in 1825), whose agent at the time of the picture was Charles Alexander. Next door is McIntyre the draper and then Downie, the wine merchant and grocer. On the left, under the key, were the premises of the ironmonger Robert Tait and those of L. & B. Walker, purveyor of baby linen, Berlin wool and fancy goods, and also agent for P. & P. Campbell, dyers, Perth. Note the coal delivery cart in the centre of the photograph.

The grocer and wine merchant George B. Downie's premises on West Port. The flat above is where he lived with his wife, Maggie. A native of Lauder, Downie had been in these premises, employing a man and a message boy, since at least 1880. The carved stone over the door to the left reads, 'In a house on or near this site James Graham, Marquis of Montrose, spent the night before the Battle of Philiphaugh on 13 September 1645, "A Candidate for Immortality"'. The left window display is replete with MacFarlane Lang, McVittie & Price and Crawford's biscuit boxes, whilst that to the right is filled with liquor, including, presumably, his own 'famed Forest Blend Whisky'.

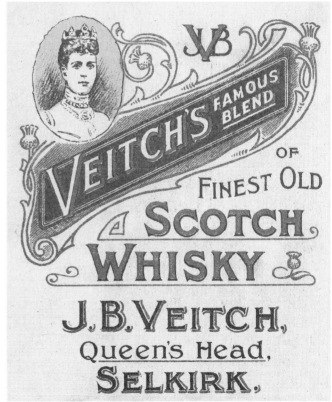

A label from a 'Veitch's Famous Blend' whisky bottle. This blend was sold by James B. Veitch of the Queen's Head public house on West Port. It was across the threshold of this pub that Robert Burns and his friend Robert Ainslie stepped like 'twa drookit craws' one May evening during Burns's 1787 tour of the Borders.

A 1909 view of the West Port, taken by the Selkirk photographer A.R. Edwards, apparently showing, on the left, the premises of the fishmonger and poulterer James Lindsay and those of the newsagent and stationer J.C. Lunt, while on the right is the Town Arms Inn which opened in 1876. However, closer examination reveals that things are not quite what they seem. In the lower left corner, the words 'West Port, Selkirk' have been partially erased and the trader's name 'J.C. Lunt' has been hand written on the negative over the partially erased name of the previous owner, A. Johnstone, bookseller and stationer. The photograph was sold as a postcard and clearly this sleight of hand would have been the result of a commission from Lunt.

The Green, looking towards West Port, with the grounds of the Haining on the right and The Glebe going off to the left with the florist's shop on the corner. In the 1860s this corner was owned by the nurseryman and seedsman, William Lamb & Sons. He was followed by Stirlingshire-born William Macauley, although by the time of this photograph from about 1910, the premises had been taken over by Frank Philips. In the bottom right of the photograph is a chain horse which was used to help heavy horse-drawn loads up the hill to Market Place.

This convoy of six carts loaded with woolsacks may have turned into The Glebe before realising it was a cul-de-sac. Either that, or the available light may have better suited the photographer!

HEATHERLIE, SELKIRK.

688

A 1911 view of Heatherlie Terrace as it sweeps from Yarrow Terrace towards The Green, the West Port and the town centre. The first two houses on the left were later demolished, the space opening up to accommodate the blacksmith, T. & R. Keddy, who was then in the yard behind. The shop on the far side of Kilncroft, under the turret, was occupied by J. Renton. This building was erected in 1878.

A winter view of the Haining, the house in the centre, taken from the east bank of Haining Loch. Left of it is the original three-storey house with its stable block. The advocate John Pringle – elected a Senator of the College of Justice as Lord Haining in 1729 (the title came with the position) – purchased the estate in 1701. Between 1794 and 1813 Mark Pringle built its replacement, a grander affair with its graceful first floor balcony to the south and arcaded portico to the front. Plans to add wings at a later date were never carried through. The old house survived as the kitchen and servants quarters until 1943 when it was damaged by fire and demolished. The building on the far left is the new house's stable block, built around the same time.

CAMP·AT·HAINING·1911·R·C·No

The Lowland Mounted Brigade came to the Borders for their 1911 summer training camp. The Lanarkshire Yeomanry were at Ashkirk and the Ayrshire Yeomanry at Whitehaugh near Hawick, while the Lothians & Border Horse, seen here with some of their horses at a corner of their camp, were at Hartwoodburn. Arriving on Saturday 24 June, the two-week training programme for the nineteen officers, 303 men, 311 horses – and one machine gun – would consist of regimental parades, drill, squadron lectures and, in the second week, manoeuvres. Had they known what war – then only 36 months away – was to become, there may have been fewer horses and more machine guns. The L&Bs had come to Selkirk in four parties – the 'C' or Border Squadron marching from their respective stations at Hawick, Selkirk, Jedburgh and Galashiels, whilst the Haddington and Berwickshire Squadron and the Edinburgh 'B' and 'D' Squadrons arrived by special trains. Founded in 1797 as the East Lothian (Haddington) Horse, it was renamed Lothian & Border Horse in 1908.

Sunday, 2 July 1911, and having been inspected by Lieutenant-colonel Lord Binning, men of the Lothian & Borders Horse march through the Haining on their way to Selkirk Parish Church for a service conducted by the Rev. George Lawson. The following day they were involved in the main brigade field operation, a sham fight where each division represented one of the eighth-century kingdoms of Dalriada (Argyll and Ulster), Pictish territory (north of the Forth), Cumbria and Strathclyde, and the Saxon kingdom of Bernicia (Tweeddale, Teviotdale and Northumberland). The L&Bs, assisted by the Lanarkshire Yeomanry, were Bernicians, but whether they were aggressors or defenders or, indeed, whether they won or lost, is not clear.

A view across the Ettrick, taking in the 1771 Selkirk Bridge, the house Mauldsheugh, built in the early nineteenth century as the Parsonage and now the Glen Hotel, and the Congregational Church. The latter was built in 1853 as an Episcopal church, but later gifted by Sir John Murray of Philipshaugh to the Congregationalists. On the hill behind is the Priory. At the time of this early twentieth-century photograph, Mauldsheugh was occupied by the Irish-born woollen manufacturer Benjamin C. Cox, his wife Harriet, their four children and four domestic servants. He appears in the 1881 census as an unmarried 27-year-old commercial traveller, then lodging with the widow Helen Dryden in Hillside Terrace. At some point later he became a partner in George Roberts & Co., the mill owners.

A flock of sheep coming into town across Stane Brig in the spring of 1913. Work on the first bridge here commenced in May 1739 but it was breached in the 1740s, with the loss of a pier and two of its five arches. Its replacement lasted until October 1777, when it too was partly broken by a flood. Its successor, widened in 1881, and shown in this photograph, did rather better, lasting until 1977 when it too was brought down by a flood.

The Cauld, after it was breached on Saturday, 27 December 1924. Through the Friday and Saturday that week, the south of Scotland suffered a great storm with the Borders, from Dumfries to Berwick, taking the brunt of it on the Saturday afternoon, when the Cauld was swept away. A similar flood in 1898 had taken not only the Cauld, but a large part of Victoria Park. The Cauld was breached again in 1963 and demolished with explosives the following year.

Opposite: From the right bank, the apparently rickety 'Auld Wudden Brig' had carried pedestrians across the Ettrick from South Bridge Street to Cannon Street and J. & R.W. Russell's 1880-built Ettrickbank Mill for many years, but by 1904 its ability to withstand another winter of Ettrick's floods was in doubt. The debate as to whether its successor should be a footbridge or a road bridge was conducted through a committee and involved the town council and the county council. An estimate of £2,920, for a 20-feet wide road bridge, was tendered by Arrol of Glasgow, and another – of £900 for a 276-feet long by five-feet wide iron lattice footbridge, with longitudinal wooden planking – was received from the Galashiels-based contractor, Mr Hepburn.

The 'Auld Wudden Brig' to Ettrickbank Mill. The mill had been developed in the 1880s by James and Robert W. Russell of Bridge Park, on ground leased from Philiphaugh Estate. The terraced housing on Cannon Street and Bridge Street was built soon afterwards. Over the years the mill passed through many hands before being bought, in 1979, by the regional council.

Accompanied by his wife, Dr Robert William Meikle, who served as the Bridge Committee Convener, opens the new public-subscription footbridge to Ettrickbank on 16 August 1906. A native of Inverary, Argyllshire, 35-year-old Dr Meikle had come to Selkirk in the late 1890s as a general practitioner and was later an honorary captain with the Royal Army Medical Corps, serving the local H Company, 4th Battalion, KOSB. The opening of the bridge had fallen on the Meikles due to the difficulty in finding someone else. The first choice, Mr William Strang Steel of Philiphaugh, who had promised £400 towards a road bridge, had other commitments on the day and the town council, having had no fiscal input, were obvious by their absence. Despite the absences of dignitaries, the day went well and, having cut the tape, the Meikles walked across, followed by the crowd.

As this picture shows, the new bridge was *the* place to be photographed. On the opposite bank are the Cheviot Mills, built in 1864 by John and James Bathgate of Station Road, and the spinning and weaving Bridgehaugh Mills, built in 1865 by Dobie & Richardson.

On Monday, 9 May 1910, the town council formalised the arrangements for the ensuing Common Riding Festival, but what the packed chamber had come to hear was the appointment of the Standard Bearer. There were two recommendations – Andrew H. Harper of Ettrickbrae and Robert Sword, the grocer, of Back Row. Nominating Andrew Harper, Councillor William Edgar emphasised how well known he was to council members and that only by not pressing his case had he missed getting the appointment the previous year. Moving the election of Robert Sword, Dean of Guild John Currie pointed out that Sword's connection with the Common Riding surpassed that of his rival as he had ridden the Marches eight times and, in 1907, had missed the appointment of Attendant by one vote. Furthermore, he came of true Souter blood. Sword carried the day by eight votes to six.

SELKIRK. STANDARD. BEARER. AND. HIS. ATTENDANTS. 1913. R.C.

The 1913 Standard Bearer John Currie (seated centre), with his attendants (standing, left to right) Bert Lidderdale, 9 Market Place, John Dickson, 6 Buccleuch Road and John Dodds, 50 Back Row. Currie is flanked on the left by John F. Riddell, 37 High Street, and, on the right, by Thomas C. Watson, 3 Castle Street. An employee of the *Southern Reporter*, Currie – through his father Robert, a woollen weaver, and his grandfather, also Robert, an ex-Dean of Guild – 'was descended from the pure leal-hearted Souter stock'. An all-round sportsman and accomplished horseman, he rode with the Lothians and Border Horse, had ridden the Marches five times, and served the Standard Bearer Robert H. Stroh the previous year and also Andrew H. Harper in 1911.

44

The Selkirk team that won the Border Rugby League title for 1934/35.
Back row (left to right): D. Stewart, D. Wilson, R. Edgar, J. Waters, G. McGhie and T. Henderson.
Middle row: A. Stewart, R. Beattie, A. Lang, J. Williamson (Captain), A. Murray, G. Smith and T. Wilson.
Front row: S. Hunter and R. Lawrie.

The Border Football Association (Seniors) team at Ettrick Park before the kick-off of their annual match against East of Scotland Juniors, 25 April 1908. While individuals in the photograph cannot be identified, the team consisted of: D. MacPherson (of Peebles Rovers and captain), T. Welsh (Vale of Leithen), W. Ainslie (Vale of Leithen), J. Easton (Peebles Rovers), R. Marshall (Selkirk), A. Hope (Berwick Rangers), M. Thomson (Walkerburn Thistle), R. Sanderson (Peebles Rovers), J. Cowie (Duns), D. Redfearn (Berwick Rangers) and A. Russell (Vale of Leithen). The Juniors were one up at half time but, with a 75th-minute goal by Sanderson for the Seniors, the match ended in a draw.

Selkirk Woodburn Football Club were the Border Junior League Champions of 1911/12 and are seen here at Ettrick Forest Bowling Club's pavilion with the Dudley Cup.

St Mary's Mill cricket team, photographed after beating Forest Mill to win the Factory Cricket Cup on the evening of 30 July 1907. The annual knock-out competition attracted teams from most of the mills, and one from the shopkeepers, and ran through June and July. Due to 1907's poor summer weather, the final was not only late but took four evenings over the week to decide. St Mary's won by 296 runs to 104. Individuals in the photograph cannot be identified and the following list of names, and runs, comes from the newspaper report: J. Brownlee (62), J. Mathison (22), J. Robertson (7), R. Wilson (0), J. Hall (0), J. Stirling (29), W. Melrose (76), A. Emond (57), A. Murray (2), J. Palfrey (14) and J. Wright (15). In Selkirk to install new looms, two unnamed Yorkshiremen are credited with introducing the game to the town. Selkirk Cricket Club was founded in 1851.

Despite lying so close to Selkirk, the transformation of Murder Moss into Lindean Reservoir was for the benefit of Galashiels and Midlem. This 1904 photograph shows, under the guidance of the surveyors, the pipe which ran east instead of west. At a cost of £1,752, the South East of Scotland Water Board created the reservoir by damming the east end of the moss. Further work in 1936 raised the water depth to 20 feet and its area to 35 acres, allowing a volume of 50 million gallons. Poor water quality in the 1970s led to it being closed.